Fingerprints

Trinity Lemm

To my mother and father,
Dear siblings,
And four beautiful friends
Who willed this book
To become what it is.

Most importantly,
To all the boys
Who broke my heart
And forced this book
To become what it is.

This one is for you.

You are holding my heart in your hands. This is a collection of poetry written over the course of nearly four years. It is divided into five chapters. Each chapter holds a special meaning. Some poems are long. Some short. Some rhyme. Some do not. Please be careful with them. I pray you cherish them as I do. And all I ask of you is that you please be patient. My writing has grown over time. I hope you notice that too.

Chapter One
The First

Lifeline

I need a lifeline
Please come and save me
The flames in my lungs
Will not let me breathe
And the roof's caving in
As I try to sleep
But my eyes won't close
The fire's too deep
The ashes in my veins
Are about to burst
They're going to fall
And the cinders are cursed
So send me a lifeline
To forget his name
Before my whole heart
Gets caught up in flames.

<u>A Fire In My Heart</u>

There's a fire in my heart
Your blood runs through my veins
There's a burning in my throat
From words leaking in the rain
Clouds are crying to themselves
In an act of desperate despair
And blood is falling from the sky
The smell of you is everywhere
Cold ice reminds me of your touch
But you are nowhere in sight
My hopeless beating heart
Has turned black within the night
I can feel you in my bones
And I crave the color of you
Your golden skin has a burning way
Of draining my crimson true
Your kiss is rather sour
As I remember it to be
These thoughts produce my heart
To shatter every memory
I can feel your venom searing
Through my bloodstream in a blaze
I ache the ghost of you
In this foggy summer haze
Almost to my heart
Your poison takes over my being
Killing me so instantly

Your wrath of joy deceiving
Ruby red, my blood drips down
In between your fingers
As my loving heart goes tonight
And your toxin, it still lingers
There's a forest in your mind
With a deranged killer on the loose
His weapon of choice, a single kiss
Killing all with sweet abuse
Run, run, hide tonight
He's looking for you now
He'll start an ocean in your eyes
And leave you dying on the ground.

Dynamite

I gave you my heart
And you gave me yours
But what is this I see?
It's plastic and poisonous
Fake and deadly
It's a bomb that I hold in my hands
Goodbye tomorrow, I die tonight
Boom goes the dynamite.

Death Of Love

By faith we join as thy destiny lies
Destructed by errors of our wronged past
Taken apart as our flower then dies
Grown gorgeously, but not enough to last
For every great flower must die in time
Killed by the poisonous hatred of love
Leaving terror and sorrow left behind
Broken screaming at the angels above
Haunted hearts shall heal into lovely bones
And put forth a new love so strongly made
A new flower has grown upon a stone
Surely, thy flower has already grayed
Each love shall die at the hands of a knife
Love cannot escape death for a new life.

<u>A Glare</u>

A glare into your eyes

Is a quick execution.

With These Flowers

As I stand with these flowers
My sun starts to shower
From the lack of love in my heart

From the lack of love in my heart
These flowers die into art
As they release their blood

As they release their blood
These showers start to flood
And my mind becomes blank

And my mind becomes blank
From this hatred I have drank
Set into fire by you

Set into fire by you
My soul turns ice blue
As the ice and fire start to mix

As the ice and fire start to mix
As a side effect from your tricks
And my heart fails

And my heart fails
As you dig your nails
Into my chest

Into my chest
Your hands are pressed
And the pressure increases

And the pressure increases
As my life deceases
My eyes begin to close

My eyes begin to close
As the thorns on this rose
Break open my skin

Break open my skin
Let my head spin
Coming from you, it's like a drug

Coming from you, it's like a drug
Pull the plug
That's keeping me alive

That's keeping me alive
Your love thrives
In my veins

In my veins
You've taken the reigns
But you decided to go

But you decided to go
As showers turn to snow
And she kisses your cheek

And she kisses your cheek
As this rose leaves a streak
On my fragile heart.

As I stand with these flowers.

Because Of You

You just stood there
Watching me drown in my own blood
Telling me to just stand up and breathe
Well how am I supposed to breathe
When all the blood is suffocating me?
How am I supposed to find the air in my lungs
To tell you what is happening
When they're full of blood
And that it's all because of you?

<u>What I Want</u>

Give me what I want

I want to sit next to you as we watch the sunset

And I hear you whisper

"I love you"

Into my ear

Give me that

No matter how fake you're letting it be.

Smoky Eye, Hazel Hue

Smoky eye, hazel hue
That rips off every dream
So ordinary, but with you
It's never what it seems
Good is bad, and bad is good
This thought has run me dry
A forest with no wood
It's all been burned alive
Smoky eye, please fix this mess
I'm standing in the ash
Ruining my new white dress
Surrounded by a flash
Hazel hue, please pull me free
I'm burning to the ground
Nothing left, nothing to see
Nobody else around
Not my choice, but by yours
As we fade from one to two
Driven by the rusty shores
And killed by someone new
Smoky eye, hazel hue
That tears apart my sanity
Leave me be, but leave me true
Don't lessen my own vanity
But it's too late to save me
I'm already charred to death
Our love has to agree
Since it started the flaming breath
But if I ever love again someday

A smoky eye with a hazel hue
It could never be the way
That I once loved you.

<u>Pretty White Lies</u>

I want your pretty emerald eyes
To look right into my brown ones
And I need you to tell me that you love me
And let those pretty, green eyes
Match your pretty, white lies.

<u>Clarity</u>
Just a little hint of clarity
Will keep this love alive
Those promises you swore to keep
In this vortex as they thrive
For one more day will never go
This thought is all that's true
As winter rolls ahead of us
And skies no longer blue
Just a little hint of clarity
Will save us all from death
But little did she know
Of the glass inside her breath
The moon tonight is all we have
In its fullest life, we see
But it's cloudy on this winter night
What happened to clarity?

The Dart

You strapped a target on my heart
Practiced on your aim
Took your shot with the dart
And smiled at the game.

A Bullet

And some words are like

A bullet going through my chest

But I would much rather be dead

Than live in a world of silence from you.

<u>Cravings</u>

Her heart wants him
Her mind is saying no
And her soul is screaming both.

<u>Touch</u>

You touched my hand

And yes

Sparks oozed off of our skin

But there was something

So right about them

That made it feel so wrong

And it was my veins that realized

That my heart did not light on fire

From that touch

What a shame

That our love is filled with so much

That it's filled with nothing at all.

The Death Of Me

The simplicity of elation
Can break open our hearts
Leaving us in leather bands
And redly tainted parts
Breathing, breathing happily
Big and healthy breaths
Can lead to horrid ire
Or loving both our deaths
I'm soaring through this love
But my affection is a pest
You back away so swiftly
From my wrath of which is best
Living in your words
And tearing in your memory
Dreaming of your emerald eyes
And drowning in this remedy
Love delivers passion
And with that, I cannot walk
The intensity of misery
And silence in your talk
I walk away to come right back
No matter how bad it ends
This game you play is complicated
Too many twists and bends
But I always play again
After time and time of losing
Bleeding here and bleeding there

Watching all this bruising
Half beaten, half dead
I stand on both my feet
Each lie you give is one more hit
But I won't live in defeat
Push me down and break my bones
They're all for you to save
Collect and burn my loyalty
Take it to your grave
I look by and there you are
You're everything I see
Loving you just this much
Will be the death of me.

Back To Hell

You grabbed my hand

And for a second

I thought it was out of love

But then I thought again

And I realized you were trying to lead me

Back to the hell you brought me to

Before this moment.

But little did you know

I'm so much smarter now

That I'm the one leading you

To the hell you deserve.

Chapter Two
The One

Let Me Run

There's dim windows and doors
In this small, enclosed space
As grey light shines through
On your pretty, little face
Kiss my hand with a dash of faith
And allow thunder to scream
Keep your lips across my cheek
As we're scolded with heavens beam
Our tongues graze upon the words
I've been desperate to hear for days
I'm confused on what I want
But I know it's your lips I love to praise
If you so need to touch and jump
Do as your body needs
I love you maybe just too much
To let you finish your dirty greed
You've already taken my heart
And it knows its precious end
But please at least let me run
Before the sins start sinking in
I haven't done completely wrong
By the Bible it tells me all
But my goodness, your eyes are sacred
And your frame, it makes the call
I must depart but must return
As my heart so longs for more

Is it my heart he really desires
Or his wanting he cannot ignore?

Let There Be Fire

So let there be fire
In this godforsaken heart
A tragedy unraveling
A bloody goring start
Am I smiling or just crying
As this fire takes a toll
A rushing moon of royalty
As you bury my body whole
Back and forth of love and hate
You sing me a sweet song
But the words are filled with sin
And my bloodstream is nearly gone
Put out the fire and save me now
I'm plunging through the floors
Help me out of this endless game
Of broken hearts and wrongful doors
You show no signs of mercy
As you make your final choice
A drought of dust and embers
Lay among your fragile voice
I look into your eyes of flames
And watch them burn like crazy
You use them as your lighter
As you blaze my eyes of daisies
One last flower here by birth
Your mother would be ashamed

You killed the only girl you had
But your sanity is at blame
One last kiss for bad reasons
Your careful mind compels
All I asked was for your love
But all you've given me was hell.

The Smell Before Rain

But you are the smell before rain

A flirtatious, little feel

Flowers growing anxious

And the animals grow real

The smell does not last long

For you are not as you seem

Looking like an angel

Though a killer in a dream

Betrayal is the spirit

Of your awful glowing heart

Your lies ricochet off houses

As you kiss my hands of art

A dancing sun grows weak

Under your powerful, young touch

And your weary darkness sets in

Your words cut through at much

The rain is coming down smoothly

And the scent of you is gone

But next time it arrives

The blood will drop at dawn

You are the smell before storms

The blood that's in my veins

You kiss and hurt and kill

But darling, we're all a little insane.

I Am

I am fuming

With the memory of what this relationship was

And the regret your words turned into

I am crying

With the confusion

Of a child who is lost and scared

I am screaming

With the hollow voice of a crow

That is a demon in disguise

I am bleeding

With the blood of a saint

At the hands of its enemy

And I am pleading

With the eyes of a lover

To her one and only.

<u>50 Feet</u>

You're standing

50 feet away

But I can still feel your hands

Around my neck.

The Day Our Love Died

Today was the day our love died out
As the words bleed onto my hands
Each syllable is its own punch
As you keep composure for your demands
I could have sworn that you were good
But darling, of course you're not
We burned the only love we had
With lips of lies so hot
Feelings of anger and disgust
Flood through my empty head
Where your hands used to lay
Has turned into a space of something dead
It seems this story was over
Before it ever began to be
This dream we had has faded
And twisted itself into a tragedy
I watch as your echoing eyes
Those glowing, green drones
Have nothing left upon them
For emeralds turn to stones
My heart stops in my chest
As your words are like a knife
Stabbing and stabbing recklessly
As you take my only life
I know you did not mean to
And I know your love was gone
And I really hoped you weren't like him

But oh god, I was wrong
You promised me months ago
That you wouldn't leave my heart
But I cannot stop you now
For your words are flames of art
I stand with tears upon my eyes
And mind and heart and soul
But you seem fine as tears don't fall
Upon your perfect face of gold
I feel myself painfully dying
As my body suffers this heart attack
Because all you did was walk out the door
But you didn't even look back.

120

And when I'm on the ground

And I'm crying at two AM

And I want to scream your name as loud as possible

And I want to call you

And I want to tell you that I love you

But I can't

Because I'm drowning in words

That won't leave my lungs

I'm lost in a forest

Filled with words for trees

I'm in a place where words aren't coming

When all I want is for them to

So when my mind is shaking

And my blood is freezing

And my heart is splitting in half

When words won't come off my cold lips

They course through the rest of my body

And inflame every inch of me

And they run from my toes to my hands

And out of my pen

And by the time I'm done

Writing out my soul onto paper

Two hours have already passed

120 pure minutes

Of writing the same word

Over and over again

In different forms and different letters
In different verbs and different nouns
And by the time I realize it
Your name has already found its way
Onto my paper
120 times.

<u>Hot Magma</u>

I don't understand why it had to end like this
We had something so extraordinary
Why did it end in a layer of hot magma
Instead of a thin layer of snow?
Why did it disappear
In the middle of the ocean
Instead of within the air around us?
We both may have deserved for it to crash down on us
But our love never deserved that
Because it wasn't about how you treated me
Or how I treated you
It's about how we treated what we had
With such a horrid elegance
And that's the tragedy within everything
We both screwed up.

You might have pulled the trigger
But I was the one who gave you the gun.

The Fireball

But thinking about you makes the fireball in the sky hotter
And it casts its light upon me
With such an elegance that you can't be mad at it for
My thoughts are forcing the wind
To swirl through the trees
Making them rumble
My thoughts produce the clouds
To rip themselves in half
And part their separate ways
And the sky is crying tears of blood
And the air is sitting in a hot remedy
Of passionate malice
And the waves get stronger with each thought
And they crash down with anger
And the water is getting so filled with hatred
That the boats upon it are sinking
Can't you see that the world hates when I think about you?

<u>Temporary</u>

I write

Because even though

You were temporary

Words are permanent.

Always

I guess for you
It was always her
And for me
It was always you.

You're Using Me

You only come to me

When you realize

That I'm the only one

Who has the water

That can put out the fire

Within your soul.

Create And Created

I am a writer

I am an author

I create

I created a love with you

And then I created a life without you

Our story is just the way

The words bled onto the paper.

Blankets

I'm trembling beneath blankets
Of your cold and icy sin
And although you are gone
I feel you pulling me back in
Because frostbite burns my bones
And our love has gone ablaze
A dust bowl of wrong choices
Marks a break upon our days
Your eyes light me on fire
And your words are on my hands
I'm too young to feel the worry
But you clearly don't understand
You broke my walls and hurt my heart
But you believe I am to blame
How am I the deadly killer
When you're the one that's so insane?
Don't come back, please stay away
I want to breathe again
But at the same damn time
I just want to feel your skin.

<u>Don't Walk Away From Me</u>
And it took a few minutes for me to realize
I was watching you walk away
I was letting it happen
Your feet moved quickly
But your soul moved slow
And I sat there wondering
If I screamed your name
Would you even turn around?

Sticks And Stones

Sticks and stones

May break my bones

But only you

Can break my heart.

Seashells

I walked along the shoreline

With you in the back of my mind

So I collected seashells

And by the time I knew it, I had 7 shells

And each one resembled you in some way

One was lighter colored

Like your skin

Another had a green tint

Like your beautiful, grassy eyes

One was filled with sand

Like your colorful personality

One was striped

Like your mood swings

One had a chip in its side

Like your heart

Another one looked almost rusty

Like your soul

And the last one had all of the above

And I sat there looking at them

Observing them

Studying them

Holding them

As if they were you

And then it hit me

Wow

I really do look for you everywhere I go, don't I?

Similar Bones

You said you were not like him
You said you weren't the same
But the only difference between you
Is the difference in your names
Your minds are both vicious
And your mouths are just to sell
Your souls are full of lies
And your hearts are full of hell
You both take but never give
And kiss but never love
You both kill me in my sleep
And act like an angel from above
You are nothing but the hole
Beneath this hollow world
The hole within your eyes
And the hole inside this girl
You both cannot be trusted
Like a flame within a home
A secret doubt inside me
Leaves a sky that is unknown
Keep your lips to yourself
And leave my soul alone
I'm running from connected twins
With different skin, but similar bones
You said you were not like him
You said you weren't the same
But I am only half a person

And you are both to blame.

<u>I Went Under</u>

I told you the first day I met you

That I didn't know how to swim

You told me to trust you in the water

You told me you wouldn't let me go under

                                          But this freezing cold water

                                          Is rushing through my bones

                                          And if you leave tonight

                                          I'm sure to drown.

<u>The One</u>

I knew from the moment I met you

That you weren't the one

I didn't expect to magically find the one

At such a young age

And I certainly didn't expect it to be you

I never wanted it to be you

I really never hoped you were the one

I just wanted you to be someone

And trust me, you were.

How Dare You

You still asked for my love

While you had her hidden in your heart

You kissed me a million times

But had her on your mind every time our lips met

How dare you.

The River

You're the river where the blood flows
The dying love that's in my heart
You're the dust that's in my bones
And the destruction of fine art
You're the star that is exploding
The dancing that has ceased
You're the shimmer that is fading
And the paper that's been creased
You're the rain that comes upon me
The crow outside my window
You're the hill I can't get over
And the ache that only grows
You are only bad within my mind
But my heart tells me to stay
I cannot make you love me more
Or change reflections in any way
But I hope one day you miss me
And I hope one day you cry
Because you sent this love to hell
And you let our hearts die
You're the river where the blood flows
The crimson in my cheeks
But the truth is that this love has died
And it's been dead for weeks.

<u>Two Cars</u>

The most painful moment

Wasn't when you left me

It wasn't when I started having flashbacks

Of us being happy

It wasn't when I stopped receiving texts and calls from you

It wasn't even when I saw you with another girl

The absolute most aching feeling

Was when I asked if you still loved me

And you looked at me

Didn't say anything

And then looked away

In that single moment

The world stopped spinning

And I heard my heart crash down on the floor

And shatter into thousands of pieces

It sounded similar

To the distressing screeches and screams that you hear

When two cars collide head on.

These Pages

And oh God

I hope you're reading this book right now

I want your fingerprints to be all over the pages

And not just in the words.

Walk Away

I like having things

I like buying hundreds of dollars worth of things

That I don't need

Because things can't get up and walk away

Like people can.

My Very Last Breath

And it wasn't until I was on the ground

Crying until my eyes nearly bled

Yelling until my throat nearly exploded

Screaming the words

"HE'S STANDING IN A DIFFERENT STATE RIGHT NOW

AND I CAN STILL FEEL HIS HANDS

AROUND MY NECK"

No, he never physically hurt me

Not once did he ever wrap his hands around my neck

But I wake up every night

To the sound of my lungs gasping for air

Because all he does is haunt my dreams

And my thoughts

He slowly finds his way into my mind

And with every thought

Every picture

Every memory

The hands on my neck get tighter

And tighter

And tighter

And one of these times

I'm going to die from it

I'm literally going to choke to death

On my own thoughts

And it wasn't until I was nearly dead on my floor

When I realized

I can run to a different state

But you still always find me
And now I'll use my very last breath
                              To tell you that I still love you.

<u>Violin</u>

"Wow, he played you like a freaking violin"
And suddenly
Music sang in my ears
A classical sound
The song of death
As I forgot to breathe, I blurted out
"I know. Don't remind me."

But damn, I can still hear it.

<u>And If One Day</u>

And if one day she breaks your heart

Like you broke mine

Then just know

That you got what you deserved.

Into The River

You drove a car into a river

While I was in the passenger seat

You set a bridge on fire

While I was standing in the middle of it

You cut a rope into 24 pieces

While I was hanging on by a thread

And right when I walk away

You come running?

You apologize

You plead for me to stay

You fall to your knees

In a bundle of false agony

Begging for one more chance

But after so long

The silence within me breaks

And the bells ring

And the sirens blare a song so loud

That people across the ocean could hear it

I yell

I scream words that have been stuck beneath my skin

Jabbing me to try to get free

I scream so violently that the leaves fall off the trees

And run away from their homes

Even though it's summer

I scream the truth that buries itself

Deep within the arteries of my heart

Drowning in red water

Sugar sweet, silver coated
Crimson bearing bullets
Escaping my mouth
Because there's nothing you can say or do
Drowning is permanent
Third degree burns don't heal quickly
Scars still dance among my hands
I held onto my seatbelt as you plunged that car
Into infested waters
So fast, yet slow enough for you to escape that car
Before I even had the chance to
I held onto the edges of that bridge
As flames glided their way to my feet
I held onto that damn rope
Until my knuckles turned a ghostly hue
And I was cut off
Sent into the abyss
I held onto you
Until it eventually killed me.

When I See You

My heart still races when I see you
But only because you bring out
The greatest hatred
My body has ever known.

What A Mistake

They told me to run

"Run from what?" I would say

"The darkness" They would reply

I did not understand

But oh God I wish I listened.

The devil chased me with a rose in his hand.

What a mistake.

<u>Catch Me</u>

Loving you is the equivalent
Of jumping off a building
And trusting you to catch me
A thousand feet later.

Sugar

Lawless lips danced upon me
With a taste of maroon greed
Cracking skulls and shredding hearts
A drought filled with a need
Each kiss is its own bullet
Covered in sugar and strings
My ribs tried to block my heart
But it can't deny sweet things
Torture never tasted so good
A drug of light desire
Running from a mix of love
And hatred can start a fire
Addiction begins with you
And with your parted rim of death
Nicotine could not compare
To the cigarette of your breath
Ripe and rushing rain
Soaks into my fragile skin
Boiling me from the inside out
Why'd I let your poison in?
You serenade me with words
That spit canons into my ears
An explosion of dusty malice
From the charcoal of a year
Sweetness pulls me down
To my knees of a bloody bandage
Sure, glass can cut me deep

But your lips do just as much damage
You've ripped my skin off edges
And now I've fallen even further
I thought that you were different
But even salt looks like sugar.

Rid You

If I could rid you from my memory
And burn your fingerprints
Off of every skin cell of mine
That you've ever touched
I would.

Lost My Breath

I walked outside today
And I lost my breath
Because even though you're long gone
Green embers of your eyes
Still trickle on the trees.

<u>Amour</u>

I fell so quickly in amour with you

Just to fall out of it

Even quicker.

Footprints And Leaves

I don't understand

Why you left with no explanation

You were here one second

And gone the next

And now tears are blurring my eyesight

And burning my skin

My throats feels like it's slowly and quietly closing

I wish I could run to you

And jump into your arms

Like I used to be able to

My hands are lonely without yours

My lips physically miss yours

My eyes ache at the thought

Of looking into yours

Because I miss you so much

I'm in pain without you here

I know I deserve better than you

But I don't want better than you

I just want you

But now you're gone

You went away like footprints in the snow

You departed like the leaves on the trees

I just want an explanation

But like footprints erase

And leaves disintegrate

I guess I should just leave it alone

And let nature do its job.

Don't You Dare

Don't you dare ever tell me

That you meant nothing to me

Damn it, I wrote a whole book about you

I wouldn't call that nothing.

Before I Bled Out

When I met you

You had your right hand intertwined with mine

And your left hand behind your back

I knew you had a knife in that left hand

I knew that somewhere along the line

You would swing it around from behind your back

And plunge it into my heart

But I ignored that thought

I pretended that it wouldn't happen

Because I liked the way that your hand felt in mine

Warm, soft

When our hands touched

There was a gentle spark

A kind collision

But as your knife went through my chest

Half a year later

There was an explosion

And even when I was dying on the ground

With a sickening wound plastered upon me

I still held onto your right hand

Because I wanted it to be the last thing I felt

Before I bled out.

<u>Unknown</u>

You look somewhat familiar

But I do not recall your name

You look at me as if you know me

Am I supposed to know you?

Every Single Blow

And in this moment

She didn't know what to do

Because her heart literally got gruesomely

Ripped out of her chest

And thrown on the floor

And hit with an axe

Over and over again

And she felt every single blow.

<u>Inside My Nightmares</u>

Dreams die among gravestones
And fire sings me lullabies
Nightmares grin within me
Because you're all that I despise
You taunt me with a ghost
That lets evil laughs glide
Touching me just so gently
With nowhere to run or hide
Why do you think it's fair
To leave my soul in real life
Yet haunt me in my dreams
A chase of rusty knives
Where blood echoes love
And someone screams my name
I cannot tell if it is you
Or if it's hell that I should blame
A thousand lyrics extend your hand
Your mouth is sinning much
I try to keep myself together
But it's hard not to miss your touch
Golden brown, a dying wish
When green eyes mess around
God, it's not fair of him
To leave me bleeding on the ground
Stubborn roses and stubborn thorns
Rest upon your smile
Inside my nightmares, I dream of you

But haven't seen you in a while
Someone wake me up
Before he kills me once again
These reoccurring promises
Have burned my lovely skin
I try to stay awake at night
To avoid your slight remover
But I can't escape your blades
I guess that you're my Freddy Krueger.

<u>Burning Buildings</u>

But if you were trapped in a burning building
And the doorknob was too hot to touch
And the flames were falling into place
Preparing to suffocate the clear oxygen
And wanting to scrape into your lungs
If there was a window to your left
With a 24-foot jump
Would you take the fall?
Would you take the opportunity?
Knowing that the love of your life
Was on the other side of that door?

But little did you know
That they were the one
Who started the fire.

Let me give you a hint—
They're not in that building.

They're standing outside of it
Watching you burn.

Fade

Memories eventually fade

But fingerprints always stay.

<u>Our Scent</u>

But we don't smell like roses anymore

All we smell like is death.

<u>Broken Knees</u>

My knees still bleed
From falling on them every night
Screaming to the moon
To bring him back to me
And yelling at the stars
To stop laughing at me.

But like him
They didn't listen either.

From The Sky

Because of you
The sun is crying
And we are all in danger.

Flames are falling from the sky
And they have your name
Written all over them.

Redrum

There's something in your hand
A weapon with wishes and shots
Your eyes were a dirty axe
With dried envy and bloody thoughts

>But later I soon found out
>That that envy reflected off her
>This jealousy turned to actions
>And these actions turned to words

And for the blood, a mess you see
All over your dirty hands
You're proud of what you've done
As the chaos then expands

>The last thing I saw before I went
>Was the red inside your heart
>The hatred in your eyes
>Is what tore my soul apart

If I were still alive
You still would've gotten away with it
My love for you was just too strong
To let this fire finally be lit

>This redrum idea is dangerous
>A nightmare in a dream
>A death beneath the blankets
>Of what redrum really means

You act as if you're innocent
From a smile thrown with care
But this crime was too important

So you thought that you should share

                        You kicked and bit and tore
                        As I screamed and begged and cried
                        The blood was thick as envy
                        And as fast as you had lied

How dare you break me open
And send my heart crashing to the floor
Bleeding out, all I wanted
Was to touch you just once more

                        But no mercy was shown for me
                        As you soaked your clothes in blood
                        Red here and there and everywhere
                        A sea of red to flood

Yet there you are so happily
With your hands around her waist
And my blood still stains your fingers
Can you tell me how sinning tastes?

                        She assisted you in my death
                        And in my blood, she spelt her name
                        You were the one with the axe
                        But she is just as much to blame

With sins splattered across you
And my blood upon your skin
You try your best to hide your hands
But darling, we all know where they've been.

Jealousy Burns

I'm jealous of the night

The way it gets to wrap you up and kiss you

Before you fall asleep

I'm jealous of the wind

How it gets to run its fingers through your hair

The way I always loved to

I'm jealous of the rain

Because it gets to feel your skin

Whenever it chooses to

I'm jealous of the air

For being able to be the one

Whom you breathe in everyday

I'm jealous

Simply and strictly envy

Of the way the world gets to watch and feel you live

Without me.

Turning Tables

If you were to ever come back

And you got on your knees

And begged for my heart back

I would simply laugh in your face and say

"I dropped to my knees every night

For months

Begging for you

And each time, all you did

Was laugh and walk away

What makes you think turning the tables

Would make it any different?"

<u>Whisper</u>
And even on the brightest of days
When I stand among the roses
Breathing in the warmth of the sun
The wind still has the guts
To whisper your name.

Remembrance

But when every single thing I look at

Reminds me of you

What do I trust?

                                                           I mean damn it

                              Even the knives look like your fingers.

Lips Of An Angel

You speak to me with lips of an angel
But you look at me as if you'd kill me
And I think that's what scares me so much
Knowing you have the body of an angel
And the heart
Of a demon.

I Swore

They said I was going crazy

They said I was broken beyond repair

And simply heading towards insanity

But I denied it

Even when the world halted for just a second

Long enough for me to realize

That the trees resembled your eyes

And that the oceans tasted like your skin

Even when I cried for days straight

Staring at my phone and every piece of you that I could find

I was falling through the floor

And the stairs shook when I walked upon them

The ground s p l i t

                                                        in half

                                          Mocking my heart

                     I could not go anywhere or do anything

                              Without breaking down

                  Because you took everything away from me

                                              My heart

                                              My light

                                           My sanity

                                          Everything

                Intelligence was no longer a key of survival

                                Walking through the fire

               And coming out stronger on the other side

Did not matter
All I wanted was to walk into the fire
And never come out of it
I was in the state of mind
Where the stars no longer appeared
And the leaves no longer turned green
My heart slowly stopped when you said goodbye
And it hasn't started back up since
No matter how many times I said I was okay
No one believed me
And they probably shouldn't have
They noticed how my eyes would glow of flames
When looking at pictures of you
And how I would scream bloody murder
And rip my hair out at the sound of your name
They all noticed
And they all knew.

They accused me of losing my mind
But I swore I was fine.

Fire Or Water

Your eyes were an ocean

But your mouth spat fire

And I couldn't decide

If I was drowning or burning.

<u>A Thousand Reasons</u>
I can find a thousand reasons
Why you left me
But I can find a thousand more
About why you should've stayed.

<u>Every Flaw</u>

You judged me for every single flaw that I had

Yet you were cold

From your fingertips

To the center of your bones

And I never judged you at all.

A Hated Body

I hated my body

Not because I did not like its shape or size

But simply because

It is not the same

As when you touched it last.

<u>Forget Me</u>

Forget me

Forget that I was ever lodged in your brain

Forget that I ever existed in your heart

And swam in your veins

Forget that we ever drove with my hands on the wheel

And your foot on the gas

Forget that our skin ever touched

Forget that whenever I was rambling on

You'd smash your lips against mine to shut me up

Forget that I was the first girl you ever loved

Forget that we went on countless adventures together

Testing the world and all that's inside it

Forget that our eyes dwelled so deep into each other

Forget that Heaven brought us together

Just forget it

Forget about me like I've forgotten about you.

<u>An Empty Chest</u>

It wasn't until your eyes turned cold

And I stuck my hand inside your chest

And tried to find your heart

Because lately, it's been quiet

My hand searched and searched

And I froze in place

As I realized the stone cold, bitter truth

And I finally thought to myself

"Oh my God

I've been listening to a heartbeat

That was never actually there."

No wonder why you took so many hearts.

You needed them to fill the empty hole in your chest.

Lifeless

If only you knew

How lifeless you made me feel.

The Deepest Wound

You cut a wound in me

So

D

E

E

P

That even hell winced at its sight

And then just as I thought you were going

To kiss it where it hurt

And then wrap it in a bandage

You poured salt all over it

And told me that if I screamed

You would leave me

And so I kept my mouth shut

Even with the worst pain I've ever felt

Rippling through my body

I kept my mouth shut

When I wanted to scream so loud

That the heavens would shake

I kept my freaking mouth shut

To keep you from leaving

And you left anyways.

<u>Your Hands</u>

Go ahead

Throw your claws over my skin

Scrape into my heart

Pick it apart

And beat it to pieces

If your hands are the ones doing it

Then I don't mind.

Until The Moon

I'll write about you until the moon disappears

And the sun shatters

Because even though it's summer

No matter how green the world is

Each petal and leaf is dying

Spilling brown blood upon the ground

Until all that's left in my eyes

Is your name written in the clouds.

But even those are dead too.

Broken Floors

Eyes wash up upon me

You control me with your pen

I pray to God to keep my floor

From falling through again.

The Only Answer

I knew I loved you

When the minute I stopped smiling

You were the only answer.

24 Steps

And so there I was

                                              Alone, again

Walking through hundreds and thousands of feet of grass

The grass was wet from the sweet morning dew

Similar to how your eyes

Once glossed over when you saw me

But the coldness of the air

Flashed me back to the coldness of your eyes

On the day you left

Reality

And so I walked on as if it was ordinary

That I was walking through hundreds of gravestones

Searching for one specific one

My heart raced slightly

An intense feeling covered my shivering skin

Maybe I was getting closer

I checked each headstone one by one

Hoping that I would come across

The one I wished to see

None of them were what I wanted

Maybe if you hadn't left that day

I wouldn't be here right now

Searching

By myself

Unwanted and worried

Broken and scarred

I was about to give up

To turn around and go home

But something inside me

Willed me to take 24 more steps

Just 24

So I did

And there it was

The memorial I had been hunting for

I bent down to get a closer look

I wiped off the dirt and debris upon it

To make its desolate letters clearer

And I sat there

Collapsed on the ground

Crying tears of heartbreak

For what seemed like a whole 24 hours

And I just kept reading it over and over

"Here lies our love

May it forever

Rest In Peace."

Immediate Love

I knew my lips would love yours
Long before they ever even touched.

But now they'll never touch again.

History

I was always silver to you
While you were always my gold
You danced in my bloodstream
While turning it ice cold
Eyes flickered, fire burning
And lit me up in flames
Matching all the forests
And the crashing of the planes
Now you act like I'm a stranger
Holding a gun to your head
When the tables were always turned
Yet a knife was held instead
To my throat, oh to my throat
It was there for way too long
You may have the power physically
But I'm mentally too strong
I was there and you know it
I left a mark on you
I sprinkled myself into your veins
In an effort to fix the view
You can walk away and not look back
But I'll always be in your mind
Hiding between the bruises
Of the choices you designed
So make that devils grin like you do
From sea to shining sea
But we both know damn well

You can't erase history.

The Swings

I noticed how the swings were all empty

Yet they still moved a gentle swing

They looked lonely

It was almost as if they were missing someone

And they had to mimic the way

They used to move happily

When loneliness wasn't the devil.

Summer Has Arrived

The trees are green
The water's warm
And the sun is back
But you're not.

And I don't think you ever will be.

Come back.

<u>I Am Drained</u>

The heat of you drains me

And writing about you drains me

And running from you drains me

And thinking of you drains me

And everything about you drains me

But nothing drains me more than loving you.

<u>Tuck Me In</u>

Your presence soothes me to sleep

Better than any lullaby ever could.

Purity

Even the clearest of water

Doesn't taste as pure as your skin.

Oncoming Trains

People like you disgust me

So when I saw a young girl being pushed around

By the hands of someone

With the same icy blue skin as yours

I cringed

And I bolted towards her

I barely know this girl

And I'm running in front of oncoming trains

To save her

Because I just wish

That someone would've ran in front of oncoming trains for me

When I was the one

That was tied to the tracks.

Petals

Petal one

He loves me

His irises dig deep into me

Burying all the love they possess

His loving skin touches mine

As our hands fit so perfectly

Hearts beating together

Lungs breathing together

He loves me.

                                              Petal two

                                      He loves me not

                        He spits toxins down my throat

                And shatters every bone in my body

                                  I cannot breathe

          As his hands fit their way around my neck

                                        And squeeze

                    He is killing me and he knows it

                                    He loves me not.

Petal three

He loves me

Apologies flicker out of his mouth

And he kisses every piece of me

To remind me of his precious love

A sign of the way our hearts are supposed to touch

And his irises are there again

Sending notes to my brain
He loves me.

                                  Petal four
                          He loves me not
      Again, I find his hands around me
          About to burst open my heart
         He craves to see my aorta break
        He wants the power of controlling me
             And so he gets what he wants
My death gives him more than enough power
                         He loves me not.

Petal five
He loves me
Gentle hands brush over my hair
A symbol of roses dance in his cheeks
His love sparks someone inside me
That aches to feel his arms
As he whispers his love into my ear
And I believe it
He loves me.

                                    Petal six
                          He loves me not
His devotion to destruction has taken over
          And he takes it too far this time
              He splits my entirety in half

And he leaves me dead on our floor
Echoing and crying of a love that wasn't there
I really thought he loved me
He loves me not.

Most flowers only have five petals
But this rose has six.

That's just my luck.

Street Signs

Your eyes match the street signs
That lead me right back to you.

<u>Cold Weather</u>

I should've known when I met you
That you were cold
Because I touched your skin
And it was ice
I knew I should've ran
But your eyes were so warm
Compared to your hands.

I knew when I loved you
That you were still cold
The very second we stood in 90 degree weather
And your skin stayed like snow
Soft, yet freezing
Light, yet thick
I knew I should've ran
But you had already touched my heart
And made it frozen.

Despite all the hints God threw at me
I stayed.

I knew I should've ran
But it's so hard to run in the cold.

<u>I Wish I Wasn't</u>

For some reason

No matter how much poison you pump into me

I am still in love with you.

How We Ruined

I knew it was gonna end sooner or later

But I never thought it would end like this

This awful

This hateful

It disgusts me how we ruined our love

And turned it into something so ugly.

Incapable

And I think what's so sad about all of this

Is that I've been so hurt

So damaged

To the point where my heart

Physically feels incapable of falling in love again

And I think that's the worst part of it

Not how much it hurt

But how much it took

And as I stand still

I do not hear a heartbeat

No matter how much I want to

No matter how many boys walk by

No matter how many look at me as if I'm beautiful

It will not restart

How many bombs can be thrown at someone

Until their heart finally explodes?

To Live A Fairytale
Why is it so easy to write about love
But so hard to actually find it?

And Then You Were Gone

You were there

And then it started raining

A torrential downpour

And somewhere between that second

And the next

I lost you in the storm

And then you were gone.

Maybe this is why I am so afraid of water.

<u>The Only Piece</u>

Writing about you

Is the only piece of you

That I have left.

Trigger

It's like this back and forth war within me

One second, I'm fine

I'm done with him

The flowers have bloomed

The sun is healthy

He doesn't matter at all

And I feel happy

And then a minute later

My heart is yelling

Saying it misses his

And my skin yearns for him

And each flower that I've grown

Has died in the war.

Angels and demons have made a home inside of me
It only took one trigger for them to clash.

He was that trigger.

<u>Every Inch Of Me</u>

If you're so captivated by my presence

Then break me open

I dare you.

Examine the dirt within my bones

The way the white has turned into a dull grey

Where wishes were once stored

But have long ago vanished

Leaving traces of their souls

Inscribed in each cell

Each inch

My spine has disintegrated

From the burdens it has carried

The hatred it has walked upon

See how the pieces of my bones have shattered

Snapped in half

Becoming sharp weapons

Used to gash wounds into my insides.

Watch my liver

The way it washes poisons from my bloodstream

Carrying what one would call alcohol

And what others call safety

A mixture of purple and black

Because it is so dead

So tired from trying to kill off

The bad within me
So tired from trying to save me
That it couldn't even save itself.

Observe my womb
The way it began growing flowers
A gentle garden
Dreaming of various colors
Being brought upon each day
By the most pure substance to reach our earth
And raised by the power of the sun
But one by one, each one died
Each petal fell upon the dead grass
And the garden burned
Roses screamed within me
Dancing among the flames
Begging for their lives.

Notice my hands and feet
How they no longer work
My hands no longer feel
No longer touch
They have been broken
Each finger, chopped
By a knife with the letters of the word
Hatred
Spelled on it
My feet have been frozen

No longer moving
Just stuck in time of what once was
Captivated by the ground under them
Too bad they won't ever feel anything new.

Look into my eyes
They are stone
They spell out words such as help and hurt
They used to shine with the stars at night
But ever since they stopped seeing yours
They stopped
They froze
The shine within them simmered
And a certain edge of destruction came
Showing them the worst
That the world had to offer
My poor, brown eyes
Saw hell.

Read between my lips
Cracked and dry
They try to speak but nothing will come out
Suddenly speechless and unwilling
A closing throat and a drop of dust
The corners of my lips stay motionless
No smiles or frowns
No love or hate
My lips feel absolutely nothing

Besides the cold and despair

Of missing yours.

Explore my stomach

Watch it digest nothing but sticks and stones

Holes are rapidly burning

And everything is on the line

The acid within my stomach

Becomes my enemy

As if it searches for a way to hurt me

And kill me

And love me

Begging to tear me open

And threatening to escape my mouth

I do not think this diet is healthy.

Discover how my skin aches

The way each line fades into the abyss

It feels as if I cannot move

If I move, every skin cell on my entire body

Will either break or burn

It is ice cold

The deepest depths of winter

The blood behind it turns dark

Red shall no longer linger

But it will break with the rest of my skin

Tearing and breathing bullets

Pulling my skin back

To see the flesh beneath.

See how my lungs stopped
Halted in the middle of a single breath
The left lung hopes for what was
And the right lung begs for what is
But no answers wash through them
As the tubes leading to them are crashing
Water is erupting inside
And a tsunami is taking form
Air is all they need
But even the simplest things
Are too hard to get
And so they stay there
Drowning.

Study my brain
It holds demons inside of it
Wars on top of wars
Between heaven and hell
Where leaves fall off the trees
And the earth stops spinning
The moon vanishes in thin air
And the oceans sing of death
The blood inside my head
Moves on with nothing but terror
My brain is dying slowly
Incapable of speaking or thinking or living

Each brain cell is blowing away
Rushing out my nose in droplets of blood
At least my nose works.

Plunge into my heart
My aorta has bursted
An explosion has taken over
Blood is escaping
Drowning every piece of my insides in murder
Knives are stabbing away
It hurts
Why do bombs keep going off?
They slither in my veins
My arteries cry out
In such pain that it's silent
Crimson syrup glides down my body
And marks its words in a single puddle
As all of this happens in a second
Jesus, my heart was just
Trying to do its job.

Feel my soul
The way it's whispering words that aren't there
Praying for someone to save it
From this chasm of lightless torture
Enveloped in hatred and broken hearts
It is burning away
Not towards the skies or the ground

But into nothing

It feels the world disappearing

It wants life to be normal and loving

But this soul is not allowed to love

Not anymore

As it waits for a new body that will never come

Hoping and wishing for real bones

And a working liver

And a safe womb

And strong hands and feet

And blinking eyes

And talking lips

And a digesting stomach

And normal skin

And breathing lungs

And a healthy brain

And a pumping heart

But none of these things will ever come

This soul is dead

From the incredulous work

Of your drunken liver

And your opposite womb

And your wrongful hands and feet

And your dangerous eyes

And your lying lips

And your sickening stomach

And your invincible skin

And your full lungs

And your evil brain
And a heart that isn't there
Yet you still get to love and be loved
Tell me how that's fair.

If you really loved me like you claim
Then you'd know every inch of me.

So tell me what my insides look like.

Because right now, they look and feel
A hell of a lot like they did
In the same minute that you left me.

So tell me what my insides look like.

Bruised Cheek

I told you I loved you
And instead of taking in my words
And storing them in your heart
You used them to smack me in the face.

Nothing

But to be honest

I don't think anyone

Could ever tear me apart again

Not because I am somehow invincible now

But simply because

There is nothing left to tear apart.

<u>How It's Always Been</u>

I love myself

I really do

But I still love you more.

Next To Yours

I tried to like and fall in love with
At least 10 different boys
Since the day you left
I hoped they'd all give me
The same feelings you did
A heart beating faster than light
A certain fire catching in my eyes
A set of nerves that captivated my whole body
Yet, the most beautiful calmness and stillness
That ever entered the universe
A craving to throw my lips onto yours
The love my hand holds when entwined with yours
The absolute feeling of being alive
But the truth is, none of them
Gave me any of those feelings
None of them made my heart beat
Faster than it did
When it was next to yours.

<u>Stranger</u>

I can fall asleep at night

Thinking about the stranger that used to lay next to me

I can write about the memory of his hair

And the way his hands felt

Warm, yet so cold

I can describe his eyes in such detail

Even though I haven't seen them in so long

I can write sparked words about his actions

The way he walked

Talked

Laughed

I can vividly imagine him leaning in to kiss me

And I can use that remembrance

As a tool to base my heartbreak off of

I can write a whole book

About the stranger I once thought I knew.

I can turn his soul

Into the most amazing poetry

You will have ever read

But I cannot make him love me

Why would I want a stranger to love me anyways?

<u>Get Out</u>

Get out of my head

You're not welcomed here anymore

And get out of my heart

You don't belong there either.

False Messages

Their lips say "I love you"
But their eyes say "I'm lying."

Spontaneous

My writing is so spontaneous

One minute I'm writing about how I'm over you

And the next minute

I'm writing about how I'm drowning in your lies

Yet still love you

And it doesn't make any sense to my mind

But I guess it makes sense to my heart.

Oceans

I refuse to swim in the ocean
It's density scares me and I'm not a very good swimmer
But you threw me in before I even had time to stop you
And then you were gone
And now I'm in the middle of the shattering waves
That pull me under with each one
I'm tumbling within the currents of water
That's taking over my lungs
I'm beneath the surface
And I'm falling deeper and deeper into the abyss
The water is squeezing my bones so hard
They're about to break
And my blood is torn
Between freezing and boiling
Water is pouring into me faster than I can think
And just as my heart is about to drown
I realize something
I realize that I'm not drowning
God, I'm not even in the water
I am the water
I'm the endless blue ripples that fall along the shoreline
I'm the rising billow that crashes into the rocks
I'm the beautiful sight that can horribly drown you
I can kill you without even trying
I'm a mesmerizing ocean
But God knows I can be a hurricane
I hold the creatures of the deep inside of my bones

And the salt water runs through my veins
Waves glide out of my mouth when I speak
And sure I'm a pretty sight
But I like the sight of you better
You're fire
You're my opposite
My enemy
Heat is in your cheeks
And there's a sliver of destruction in your fingertips
You are blood red and a deep orange
You're a yellow sun
And you stay above me every single day
Heating me up
Mending my cold heart
And turning it into a warmer place
You're always going to be above me
And that's exactly why you'll always be a part of me
But that's also exactly why
We could never be together
You're fire and I'm water
And just as much as hell hates the stars
And as much as the clouds hold angels
We coexist
But you and I will never be able to mix
And that's when I knew we didn't belong
We weren't right for each other
As much as we wanted to be
We just weren't

That's why I can't love you anymore
I can't love you when you're a flame
And I'm the ocean.

Chapter Three
The Others

I Lost

Let's play a game.

You say "I love you"
And I'll say it back.

First one who means it
Loses.

The Spawn

He claims he needs your heart

But it's lust he demands

He prowls on the innocent

For his body's commands

You crave his love

But receive greed instead

Do not allow him

To get in your head

He's there to take you

To the depths of hell

It's his job, you see

And he's doing it well

He's an evil, young boy

With a gun for a heart

He enjoys the thrill

Of tearing girls apart

He'll leave you in ashes

With a heart to straighten

Be careful, my dear

He is the spawn of Satan.

<u>My Own Game</u>

If I could go back to the moment I met you

Or the moment I realized I loved you

I would bid myself to turn around and walk away

Or I'd slap myself in the face

Because I absolutely hate knowing

That I jumped into something

That I already knew so well

But still lost at my own game.

Your Heartbeat

Tonight, I heard your heartbeat for the first time

And I lost my breath

There was a sudden feeling of being stuck

Trapped and suffocating

Drowning in thoughts

Crying

A break in being alive

As if all the blood rushing through me

Just stopped for a second

And turned to ice

The wires in my brain

Snapped into 24 pieces

As I flashed back to the dark days

Where he left me

Again and again and again

And I just sat there with droplets of hatred

Forming in my eyes

Because your heartbeat

Is not his.

In The Flames

You warned me that fire
Was gonna burn at the end of this
But I thought I was strong enough
I thought I had enough water
To put it out
But this fire is out of my control
And now we're screaming in the flames.

<u>Gone</u>

And you'll give yourself

Again

And again

And again

In an effort to make him stay

But every time, he walks away

And you can't help but stay up all night

Laying in your bed

Crying to the world

Screaming until your lungs shake

Because you just want him

More than you want to breathe

More than you want your very own blood

To be pouring through your body

But he's gone

He left

And you can't decide

If you hate yourself or him more for it.

Pride In Love
I take pride in saying that I get to love you
Don't make me regret that.

<u>A Forever Stain</u>

But no matter who I fall in love with
A boy with green eyes
Or blue eyes
Or brown ones
It always stains me in the end
Because even long after they're gone
I can still see their eyes everywhere
In the trees and the grass
Or the skies and the water
Or the wood and the ground
They are always still lingering
Haunting me until my very last breath
No matter what
I can simply never win.

<u>A Shameful Boy</u>
It's such a shame
How you finally made me feel something again
After all this time of him being gone
After all this debris scattered across my heart
You brought me back to love
And within 24 hours
You brought me back to heartbreak
Back to the death I dreaded so much.

Why would you drag me out of hell
Just to kick me right back into it?

All I Notice

He walks past me
And all I notice
Are the shadows of the boys before him
Silently walking behind him.

That's when I should've known
To turn around and run.

<u>A Slight Stomp</u>

For my entire life

I have been wishing for someone like you

Someone with magic in their eyes

And roses in their heart

Someone with your laugh

And a sweet soul like mine

And now I'm sitting here

Crying to the trees again

Because once again

Heaven has brought me slight love

And once again

Hell has stomped all over it.

And You Never Will

The sun kisses my skin

But you don't.

A Deadly Name

Fluffy hair

Big frame

Tainted words

A deadly name

Hands of haven

A haunted praise

As you walk upon

A smiling gaze

Hold my heart

More each day

But your plan ran out

With every play

Inside joke

To rue the night

But you quickly turned

Down the fight

Here one second

Gone the next

Harmonies billowed

A silent text

And there you go

Oh what a shame

Such a pretty face

With a deadly name.

<u>Caution</u>
Just be careful
Boys like that
Are good at what they do.

Prince From Hell

How can he be your prince

If he wears horns upon his head

Has crimson colored skin

And dances through a throne of fire?

No More Than Lies

Do I regret not kissing you?

No

Why would I want my soft

Amorous

Impassioned lips

To become tainted

By lips filled with no more than lies?

<u>A Part</u>

You reminded me how awful it feels

To love someone.

So thank you for the inspiration.

You're now a part of this book.

Maybe This, Maybe That

I can't tell if I wanna cut the trees down

Or cry to them

I can't tell if I wanna scream

Or collapse for the skies

Maybe I'm just mad

That he doesn't realize I'm right here

That he doesn't realize the amount of roses in my heart

That I would give to him in one heartbeat

Maybe I'm just mad because here I am again

Writing until my lungs give out

Writing the word "love" over and over again

Maybe I'm just mad

Because he likes me

But doesn't love me.

                                                      Or maybe I'm sad

                                That the petals in my bones are dying

                            With each step he takes the other way

                                              Maybe I'm sad

                       That he's recreating the flame in my heart

                 That almost burned down the entire world

                                              Maybe I'm sad

                                       Because he loves her

                                         But doesn't love me.

All Over

The ground understands me.

It knows what it feels like
To have your footprints all over it.

<u>Pool Of Blood</u>

I barely knew you

All I knew was that you made me feel something

That I haven't in a long time

You gave me the tiniest twinge of love

And then threw me into a pool of blood.

Splinters

I did nothing but try to fall in love with you

And somehow, I ruined everything?

Don't turn the tables on me

We both know you were never here for the right reasons

And now this table is split

Right down the center

From you

Yet I'm somehow still the one

With splinters in my hands.

<u>By Choice</u>
You showed up by chance
But left by choice
And I think that's what hurts the most.

<u>House Of Straw</u>

His soft lips spell home upon me
But this house is made of straw
And I pray that no wolf or tornado
I pray that no rain or hurricane
Will knock it down.

Because all it takes is one straw out of place
And it will all come crashing down.

Too Deep

You had your smile hooked
So deep within me.

I couldn't get you out
Even if I wanted to.

The Air You Took

I liked you because you weren't him

It seemed as if nothing about you

Resembled any piece of him

And I was grateful for that

But then that sentence

That one, single, dreaded sentence

Came out of your mouth and I froze

All the air left my lungs

And it was as if I could hold a mirror up to you

And see him as the reflection

That single set of words was all it took

And now I'm running as fast as I possibly can

Trying my hardest to get away from you

Please don't run after me

Because knowing me

I'd let you catch up.

<u>To Art</u>

It's okay if you break my heart

Turn me to ash

I'll turn you to art.

<u>After Hours</u>

It wasn't until I was texting anyone and everyone

That I thought could help me

In hours that no one in their damn mind

Would be awake at

Unless they were hurting too

And I sat there

A complete mess

Pieces of my heart scattered across the floor

When I realized

My heart only knew how to handle itself

When it was in front of a pen and paper

Or in front of you.

A Damn Thing

When he's gone

And you can't feel a damn thing

Completely numb

From your skin to your bones

The air is empty

The ground is cold

And you feel dead

It's moments like these

That you would bleed

Just to know you're alive.

<u>Medicine</u>

You say he's your medicine
But medicine is only good to take
When your body needs it
Any other time than that
And it's as dangerous
As whiskey and a wheel.

You don't need him
You want him
But honey, he's not good for you.

Every Drop

It's raining

And every drop is another reason

Why I should've left

A long freaking time ago.

<u>A Drunken Mistake</u>
Don't use being drunk
As an excuse for loving someone else.

"It was a drunken mistake."

More Than Death

I think the worst is when your love is so deep
That you are actually afraid of losing that person
More than you're afraid of death
But what hurts even more
Is laying in bed at night
Knowing that they wouldn't flinch
If you were gone the next day.

<u>At The Moon</u>

And I want to blame you

I want to blame you so badly

But the world is telling me to just keep walking

It's claiming that it wasn't my fault

But it also wasn't his

That's when I looked straight at the moon and screamed

"I DON'T BELIEVE YOU!"

And the stars just laughed and said

"You're a teen

You're not supposed to."

<u>The Chance</u>

I wish I could say I miss your heartbeat

But the sad thing is

I never even got the chance to hear it.

Helpless

It's like that moment when you're driving
And all of the sudden
A deer jumps in front of your car
And you see its face as you hit it
Hopeful
But helpless.

I was the deer.

All I'm Sure Of

I never got to taste your lips

But I'm sure they tasted sweet.

<u>Someone</u>

They keep saying

"Someone will love you"

"Someone will love you"

"Someone will love you"

And my mouth always sadly responds

"I know someone will"

But my heart always sadly responds

"But someone isn't him."

<u>A Dark Gift</u>

When I first met you

I thought the most beautiful angels sent you

I thought you were straight from heaven

A divine creation

Given to me as a gift

But now I realize that you

Are straight out of hell

A fallen angel with fire for a soul

And a hole for a heart.

<u>It Had To Be</u>

You kissed my heart

Without kissing my lips

But you swore it wasn't love.

Honey To Smoke

I can't blame you for meeting her

And loving her before me

I can only blame fate for that

But I can blame you for the dust on my hands

The strings of my heart snapping in half

My hair falling off my head

Faster than the leaves fall off the trees

Since you met her

You won't love me

And every time my blood turns from honey to smoke

It's moments like these

That make me wish I never met you.

So Lively

The birds are so lively

With no idea

That I'm sitting under them

Crying my eyes out.

Failing

I can say I don't care all I want

But the truth is

My heart is failing

My soul is crying

And there is nothing that can fix me

Besides you.

But You're Not

My hands are bleeding

From hanging onto the rope

I thought you were at the end of.

Want, But Can't Have

I want you

I want your heartbeat

Pumping against my chest

Your smile

Glistening because of mine

Your soft touch

Warming every inch of me

Your tan skin

Captivating my eyes

Your hair

As I run my hands through it

Your laugh

More beautiful than the skies

Everything

I want all of it

And I think I'm just bitter

Because you don't want any of me.

Confessions

I must confess

I'm waiting for tragedy to strike

Because I need something new to write about

Maybe I should find someone new to love

But then again

I might as well take a knife

And plunge it through my own chest.

I'll get the same results.

Nothing I Write

I can write about you all day and night

But nothing I write

Can bring you back.

That Feeling

That feeling you get

When you hear something

You don't want to hear

Like the clouds are turning black

And the entire planet

Just fell out of orbit

It's almost like everything gets quiet

Just enough

For you to physically hear

Your heart breaking.

<u>A Wildfire</u>
The pain is spreading
From my heart to the rest of my body
Like a wildfire
I can feel it igniting apart every cell
The petals in my stomach are blazing away
And the bottoms of my feet are bleeding from the heat
God I am just hoping
That the firefighters get here
Before it's too late.

Softly Scared

I can still imagine your arms around me

Your soft touch

Your soft voice

And it truly terrifies me.

If someone so good

So pure

Could rip me open and then leave

Imagine what a predator could do.

<u>Two Weapons</u>

Hatred is a weapon

But so is love.

A Wave Of Fear

A wave of fear rushed over me

As he turned around

And started walking away

But this isn't a lovey dovey story

This isn't the one where I run after him

And jump full force into his arms

No

Not even close

This is the one where I turn the opposite way

And run as fast as I can

And fear engulfed me because all I could think

All I could hope

Was that he wouldn't look back

Run in my direction

Grab me by my hair

And force me to stay.

Being with him was hell

And I didn't realize it until the invisible bruises on my body

Screamed so loud that every house

Every building

Every bridge

Burned

And all that was left

Were dead roses among the ash.

Run

Before the hell he is

Lights you on fire

Run

Before the invisible bruises

Become real

Run

Before you die

Without seeing real love.

You're stuck in his grasp.

Leave it.

Chasing Dreams

They tell us to chase our dreams
But what do I do
When I go to bed
And he shows up?
A beautiful face with rough hands
And eyes that lie more than they look
How do I chase someone
Who left?
How do I chase someone
Who won't let me love them?

I can't chase him
He's too far away
But damn I wish he wasn't.

All It Ever Was

That's all it ever was, wasn't it?

A tired girl breaking her heart repeatedly

For boys who wanted nothing but the satisfaction of breaking hearts.

Cold And Dead

There's a spot in my chest

Where love and warmth used to lay

But now all that's left

Is a space of something cold and dead.

No Going Back

Do you think I'm stupid?

Did you really think that I didn't know

That he was going to break my heart?

No

I knew

I knew the whole damn time

The second I shook his hand

I knew I was screwed

I saw the future coming

And I let it come

I let it hit me in the face

So don't say

"I told you so"

Because reality is

You didn't

I was aware that my heart would be ripped away from me

And that the thought of him would suffocate me

I knew my fate was going to be this

But the second I shook his hand

There was no going back.

Send Her Home

If you see the me I've been looking for
Please tell her to come home
I can't find her anywhere
And I miss her like crazy.

A Goodbye

He doesn't deserve a poem

He doesn't deserve a paragraph

Or a compliment

Or an "I love you"

Because he fed me hatred

Coated with fake love

He shoved lies down my throat

And didn't help when I started choking

He shot me straight through the heart

Without thinking twice

There is not one demon in hell

That thinks he deserves any damn thing

Other than a goodbye.

<u>A Set Of Words</u>

Now all you are to me
Is something new to write about.

But nothing other than that.

My Pen's Fault

It's my pen's fault

That I write such dark words

Such gruesome poetry

Splattered onto red paper

It's my pen's fault

That mirrored images of death

Spell out their names

It's my pen's fault

That my heart will concave

Every time I write with it

It's my pen's fault

That my blood turns to rock

When it's in my hand

It's my pen's fault

That tears fall onto every page

I stain with its hatred.

But more than anything

It's your fault

For forcing me to pick it up everyday.

Roses Are Roses

I'm not boy crazy

I just simply have a lot of dead roses

Stuffed inside my ears

And nose

And mouth

And the gaping wound in my chest.

It hurts

And it burns

But roses are roses

So I'll take what I can get.

<u>The Earth's Center</u>

We grow up to believe that trust is earned, not given

But how can that be

When every time I meet a pair of green eyes

I swoon at their beauty

Every time I'm being held

I hold on tighter

Every time a hand grabs mine

I can't help but smile

Every time I see a pretty face

Butterflies ignite my bones

Every time I'm being hugged

My soul feels complete

Every time I steal a kiss

I kiss harder?

How come every time I meet someone new

I fall farther than the Earth's center?

I hand out trust faster than the tide rises

There is no way in hell

That trust is earned.

We just wish it was.

<u>Stuck On Something</u>

And there I was again

Thinking and wishing and dreaming

Of being with you

But that's how I always was—

Stuck on something that didn't exist.

Something that never would.

Until It's Him

I had the answer this whole time.

He doesn't care
And he's never going to care
Until he's the one drowning.

Boiling Blood

And as you walked away

I could physically feel the blood in my body

Start to boil.

Be careful

You've started a fire

That you'll never be able to put out.

<u>Fire Hazard</u>

His lips may lie with sugar on them

But you know the truth

In the back of your head

You know damn well

That those lips are actually a fire hazard.

Hope Gone Wrong

I hope I get the chance to love you
I hope I'll get to feel your skin
And kiss your heart
Just as many times as your lips
I hope I get to breathe bright air with you
Sitting among summer bliss
And taking in the sweetness of the blue skies
I hope I get to lay with you
And sleep with my head along your chest
Listening to the wondrous beat of your wondrous heart
Taking in the warmth of your soft blood as it runs through you
I hope I get to throw my hands through your hair
And feel the world lighten
As you kiss my forehead
I hope you don't leave me like the others
I hope you don't hate—

And the poem stops right there
Because before I could get another word down
An axe went straight through my heart.

The Only Choice

I said goodbye to him

And it was hard

It was so hard

But I didn't have any other option.

Chapter Four
The Only

Deadly Hands

Stop letting his hands touch you
All they do is destroy.

A Thousand Kisses

You can kiss me a thousand times
But it doesn't mean you love me
And you can say it a thousand times
But that doesn't mean it either.

Before He Left

I don't care what he's saying to you now
All that matters is what he said before he left.

On Your Doorstep

I could write paragraphs

On top of paragraphs

About how I miss you

And how I want you

And need you

But it's no use

Because your eyes will never come back

And your lips will never come back

And I'll never get to hug your soul ever again

And it rips me apart

But there's nothing I can do

You can only sleep on someone's doorstep

So many times

Before realizing

That they're never coming home.

<u>A Fine Line</u>

I love him

But there's a fine line

Between lust and love

And he doesn't seem to know the difference.

Hate That I Can't

I hate you for hurting me

I hate you

I hate you

I hate you

But God knows I don't mean it.

I wish I could though.

In The Ears

Kind words mean nothing

When you throw them around

And smash them in the ears

Of every victim you've ever claimed you loved.

Knots

Do you really think you can kiss him again

Touch him

Hold him

Knowing that her hands were all over him?

In the same places you used to put yours?

Your stomach just knotted at the thought

Didn't it?

<u>You Weren't There</u>
You can say whatever you want to now
But you sure as hell weren't there to say it months ago
When I was laying on my floor crying.

Can't Change

If you left me back then

You'll leave me again

No matter how much light ink

You try to put in my pen.

<u>The Same</u>

You're the same you

And I'm the same me

But knowing us, that's exactly why

We could never be.

Never again, at least.

<u>Then Why</u>

If we had so much in common like you claim
    Then why'd you leave?
If we were so happy like you claim
    Then why'd you leave?
If we were so good together like you claim
    Then why'd you leave?
If you cared about me so much like you claim
    Then why'd you leave?
If you loved me like you claim
    Then why'd you rip my heart apart
    And feed it to the wolves?

All My Heart Says

I can't be with you

Knowing that your hands have been all over her.

Ignored Love

You can't come back to me
And beg for me to love you again
When I haven't stopped loving you at all.

You just never noticed
Because you were too busy loving her.

Against Time

Fighting against time
Is a hard thing to do
But I did it for you anyways.

Lit Match

You lit a match

Looked me dead in the eyes

And threw it straight at me

With a smile on your face

And so I burned

I burned into the deepest ash

A pile of breaking lullabies

My skin screamed

And my lungs caved in from the smoke

I couldn't see anything besides the hell on my body

And your face on the other side.

Don't love someone who isn't afraid of fire.

We all know where they're from.

In A Bottle

He was drunk off all the souls he stole

And trapped inside a bottle.

Any Other Heart

You can't expect me to still want you
After everything you put me through
But you can expect me to still love you
Only because my heart was born that way.

If I had any other heart besides this one
You'd be shunned into hell.

Doesn't Work That Way

You can't love me

When you're off somewhere loving her.

<u>Way Too Much</u>
But I swear when the word "love" rolls off my tongue
I mean it
I mean it way too damn much.

<u>If You Love Them</u>

I don't care how hard it gets

How impossible it seems

How terrible it feels

The bottom line is that

You don't give up on someone you love.

Maturity

You claim you've matured
But maturity is being able to handle any situation
And compromise with the person you say you love
Mature and loving people don't run
When an issue arises.

<u>Even Hell</u>
There's fire in her eyes
And the flame is dancing so deep
That even hell is afraid of what she's become.

Just A Word

Sorry is not enough for me.

Do You Remember

Remember when you hated her

And loved me?

<u>Send Me Love</u>

Send me roses

And I'll let them die

Send me love

And I would let it die

If only it wasn't dead already.

Chasing Nothing

How long is it going to take you to realize

That you are just

Chasing

And chasing

And chasing

Someone that is miles

And miles

And miles away?

You are never going to catch up to them.

If You Loved

If you loved me
The way I deserve to be loved
Then maybe things would be different right now
Maybe we would still be
In each other's arms
Instead of at each other's throats.

People You Love

No

You know why you always let him stay?

You know why you always believe him?

Because everything he tells you is easier

Everything he says is easier to accept

You don't want to accept that maybe the truth

Is that he was talking to her

While he was with you

Or that he lied straight to your face

You don't want to accept it

Because it's painful

But sometimes pain

Can lead to a better you

So stop picking the easier option

I know you think he's the love of you life

But the hard truth is that he's not

He never has been

And he never will be.

You don't lie to people you love.

Trying Again

Trying to love you again
Was a mistake.

<u>Actions Are Truth</u>

You can say whatever you want

But if you don't have the actions to back it up

Then your words are completely

And utterly irrelevant.

Said And Done

You can buy me all the presents in the world

And tell me nice things that I want to hear

And apologize 2,000 times

But you cannot take back what has been said and done.

<u>Her Only Choice</u>
This is just what he does.

He grabs her heart
And pulls her in
So that she has no choice but to stay.

Conned

There I was again

Saying "I love you" to him

And there he was again

Conning me into saying something that I didn't mean.

Because how on Earth could I ever love someone

Who tore me apart?

<u>Do I Want To</u>

Every boy that I've tried to fall for
Since the day you left
Was just a distraction
A joke
An attempt to get my mind off of you
But in the end
It never worked
Time and time again
I found my mind circling right back to you
And I don't think I'll ever be able
To get out of this deathly cycle.

But the real question isn't
Can I get out of it?
The real question is
Do I want to?

Nonexistent

I loved you with everything I had
Smiles were given to you
Words were given to you
Skin was given to you
But all I got in return was a touch of fire
You were full of desire to kill
And nothing more
Every piece of me was captivated by you
And every piece of you hated me
And with every kiss you gave
Every hug
Every slight touch
I felt the fire within it
I felt the burn it gave off
And I had mistaken it for love
What I thought was a spark
Was actually a world of chaos
A world of difference
Because your heart was incapable of loving me
Even when mine loved you more
Than the leaves love the wind
Even when I needed you more
Than a set of lungs needed oxygen
Even when I ripped myself into pieces
To leave on your doorstep
Or when I wrote hundreds of poems about you
I truly gave you all

And all you gave me
Was a raindrop for every second hidden in vain
I felt way too much
And you felt nothing at all
I guess that's just how hearts are these days—
Nonexistent.

Unsee

There are just some things in this world
That you can't unsee
And seeing you with her
Is one of them for me.

I Need To Believe Myself

I don't know how many times
I've reminded myself that you're lying.

And I don't know how many more times
I'll choose your words over my own.

Eaten Alive

I sat in your arms

But it felt like I was being eaten alive.

<u>Wrong Words</u>

If you loved me like you say you did

Then you wouldn't have fallen in love with her.

A Ghost Resumes

You can't blame me for this
You're the one that bludgeoned me open
And splattered my heart against the walls.

<u>What Happened</u>

What happened to you sending me good morning texts

And tucking me in to sleep?

What happened to you kissing my forehead

And hugging me so tight that I couldn't breathe?

What happened to you smiling and laughing with me

And never letting go of my hand?

What happened to you loving me

And meaning it?

<u>Nothing Good</u>
Nothing good ever comes
Out of loving you.

Never Stopped

I never stopped writing about you

And I don't know

If that screams love or hate.

All We Are

We are not dating

We are not together

We are simply just two ex-lovers

With a forever spark

That will never again be a flame.

Brainwash

Stop letting him brainwash you.

<u>Complications</u>
          I want you so bad
      But our love is just too complicated
All I know is that with you here
          It's so hard to breathe
      But without you here
I can't breathe at all.

All I Taste

I can taste the dishonesty

Within every kiss.

<u>Part Of The Story</u>

Darling, be careful

He is a storyteller

And you are simply just

Part of the story.

<u>The Day You Left</u>

It's raining so hard outside right now

Oceans are falling from the sky

The ground is being flooded

And the trees are shaking helplessly

The animals are hiding in fear

Lightning seizes to destroy the air

And it's cold

So, so cold

It's raining so hard right now

But still not as much as it did

The day you left.

<u>Why Did You</u>
But after all this time
You came back
Now I'll spend my lifetime
Trying to figure out why.

<u>Always Yours</u>

We all know my heart

Never left your hands.

<u>All An Illusion</u>
He was throwing words at me
That meant nothing
But he knew they would make me stay.

It's like looking in a kaleidoscope.

It was all an illusion.

<u>If You Read</u>

But if you read all my poems

Would you recognize me?

Would you be able to tell it was me

From the hurt on every page

And the love in every line?

But more importantly

If you read all my poems

Would you recognize yourself?

Would you be able to tell it was you

From the descriptions of your eyes

And the demons living behind them?

It'll take thousands of poems

For you to realize

The hell you set free.

In One Word

I'll sum up our entire relationship
In one word.

Wrong.

A Constant Loss

You treated me and our love like a game

You still treat it that way

As if I'm some prize you win

And then throw in your closet

Only to forget about it

And never look at it again

I was no more than a piece of paper

A doorknob

A shirt that you wore once

And then never wore again

To you, I didn't matter

My presence would light up your eyes

For only a second

Just to bring them back to the darkness they live in

The hell they possess

I was a board game

I only mattered when you wanted me to

Other than that, I didn't exist

It was almost like to you

I didn't breathe

Unless you were standing there with me

To you, I wasn't alive

Unless you decided that I could be

You would give me love

And then take it away

You would give me life
And then throw me out a window
It was all a game to you
You have always made the rules
That's how it always has been
And for some reason
I've always let you played it
How many more times am I gonna play
Until I realize that I can never win?

<u>A Whole Lot</u>

Just think about it

There is nothing there

Besides a whole lot of hatred

Disguised by a little bit of love.

<u>A Beautiful Rose</u>
I want to write a story
About the most beautiful rose
The world has ever created
So beautiful
That people would die for it
Because it will be the closest
That they have ever been to love.

Roses In My Hands

I fell asleep with roses in my hands
And woke up
With thorns all over my body.

<u>My Type</u>

You want to know what my type is?

Boys that have brown, dusty hair

With green eyes that hold nothing but dead leaves

Hands that only cause problems

Lips that lie freely

And a mind that is so goddamn difficult

That I cannot function.

That is my type

Don't ask me why

Because I don't even know myself.

Even My Heart

I'm usually the type to give second chances
But what you've done to me is so unforgivable
That even my heart is yelling no
And that's saying a lot.

A Smile Of Lies

Your smile is drilled into my head
But your lies are drilled into my heart.

<u>No Taste</u>

With lips that have no taste

You spoke to me

But it's as if nothing was coming out of your mouth

You kissed me

But I didn't feel a damn thing besides pain.

How is it that I have roses on my lips

But you only have thorns on yours?

<u>With Every Turn</u>

But it seems like every time I turn around

I get another freaking stab wound in my chest.

Like My Heart

But all the roses I ever see anymore

Are dead.

Show Me

If you really love me

Then say it to my heart

Not to my face.

<u>Batman</u>
You can pretend you're not the bad guy
But pretending can only get you so far.

I've been in this situation a hundred times
I don't know how many more times I'll have to say it.

Batman might dress dark
But he doesn't go around breaking hearts.

<u>Regret</u>

I'll remember you, I'm sure of it
You were too important to forget
But I can't love you anymore
You've given me too much to regret.

Chapter Five
The Truth

<u>Best For you</u>
Don't blame the world
For doing what's best for you.

He was not good for you.

That's why he's gone now.

I Am Permanent

You say that you're done

And that you're leaving

You can walk out the door a hundred times

But it still won't change the way

You looked into my eyes

Or the way you kissed my hand

And cheek

And forehead

And lips

You can never look back if you want

But it still won't change the way

You begged on your hands and knees for me to stay

And now all of the sudden

I am apparently not good enough for you?

No

I am treasure

My skin is made of pure gold

And my heart is a diamond

I am worth anything and everything in this world

Don't try to make me think that I'm not

I've survived without you before

I know I can do it again

I am my own best friend

And whether or not you are here

I will keep breathing

I will stay alive because gold and diamonds never die

And I refuse to allow you to make me believe that they will

You don't truly love me

You never did truly love me

And you never will truly love me

And that's just the way you are

Lies are constant friends of your tongue

You sin more than you love

And when you are the one crying on the floor this time

Vacant of lust that pretends to be love

Don't even text me

Know that it's your own sins

That put you there

I want you to live with the fact

That I am gone

The same way that I had to live with that fact for you

You can say you don't want me all you'd like

But I'm the only me there is

My heart is the land

And my eyes are sometimes a river

But you'll remember me

There's no way not to

So when you breakdown at the sound of my name

Or my favorite movie

Or our song

Or anything that reminds you of what we used to be

Deal with it

I know I'll never fade from your mind

I am treasure

I am permanent

You lost my presence

But you will forever remember my heart and soul

I am permanent

You cannot scrub me off

You cannot pray to the heavens 24 times

You cannot wish upon a star

Because it will not work

Permanent things are not easy to get rid of

Don't call me at two a.m. apologizing

Saying that I can't get out of your head

Because all I'll do is shrug

Say "Oh well"

And hang up the phone.

Deal with it

It's your fault anyways.

The Steps

I'm worth more

Than the steps you took to your car.

<u>Bricks Or Feathers</u>

When being in love

Feels like you're carrying a thousand bricks

That's when you know

It sure as hell isn't love.

                                                        Carry feathers

                                                        Not bricks

                                                        Unless you want

                                                        Swollen hands

                                                        A breaking back

                                                        And a heavy heart.

Every Boy

Just think of it this way.

Every boy has the same brain
But not every boy has the same heart.

Interpret this how you'd like.

To Stop Time

You're not special enough to stop time

You're special to the population

To the human race

But the sun doesn't shine

Just for you

And the rivers don't flow

Just for you

You may be a beautiful creature

But oh honey

You're here to live

For the whole world

But the whole world isn't here

To live for you.

<u>Mad</u>

They searched my poetry

And they turned to me and said

"Have you gone mad?"

So I just looked at them, laughed, and said

"No. I just have a heart with hands."

Jump

I know that you're afraid to love

The same way you're afraid to swim

But he is that pool

He is the warm water

But right now, you're just walking in circles around it

Burning time

Procrastinating

All you're life, you've been avoiding the water

You've been avoiding falling in love

Jumping in love

You are afraid

Of going in and going under

But God's waters were meant to keep us afloat

All you have to do is count to three and jump.

Don't just walk away again

Feel the water wet your skin

It's one hell of a refresher.

Three

Two

One

Go.

All The Love

I gave you all the love I had
How is it my fault
That you didn't accept it?

It's not.

Unlove

You can't force yourself to love someone

And you can't force yourself to unlove someone.

Give yourself time.

<u>To Fall</u>

I didn't fall in love with him

Yes, I am in love with him

But falling means that somewhere along the line

You're going to hit the floor

And break

And when you do break

You'll have to go through the process

Of realizing that the person you fell for

Just wasn't the one

And that's how you'll know who is the one

Because you simply just walk into love with them

There is no falling

No shattering

No having to recollect yourself

And in a few steps, you'll be in love

Without ever having to fall

Just wait

Your forever

Is just steps away.

Blame

Put down your phone darling

Stop waiting for him to text or to call

Because he's not going to

He's too busy

Running his lips across her skin

Because he got tired of you

He got tired of knowing

That your soul

Was too good for his

That your heart

Was too pure for his

Because you are a diamond

A golden rose

You have everything in your heart

That he does not

So stop blaming yourself for his departure

He left

Because you were too good for him

And he knew it.

<u>Without Him</u>

You've lived without him before

You can do it again.

A Pen Or A Bottle

I'm being offered to bathe in
The bitter taste of alcohol
The feeling of the stale vodka
Running down your throat
The fuming smell of intoxication
Gasping out of your mouth
But that's not what I want
I don't want to be so drunk
That I ruin my insides
I don't want to be so tipsy
That I can't think straight
I don't want to forget about all my problems
Because yes
I have battles
Everyone does
But I would rather fight those battles head on
Sober
With my clean heart and soul
I don't need a night of "forgetting"
Because it's never truly forgotten
I want to solve my problems
Not forget about them
And I would much rather do it
With a pen in my hand
Than a bottle of vodka.

<u>Willpower</u>

Some people just move on quicker than others
It has nothing to do with how much
They love you or don't love you
It has everything to do with willpower.

Someday

Maybe he'll come back to you someday

But today is not that day

And you have to accept that.

Opposites

You know how they say opposites attract?
Well they're right
Opposites do attract
But the ironic part is that opposites
Can never love each other unconditionally
No matter how much hope
Their infatuation brings
Because think about math or chemistry
After all
Two positives make a positive
And two negatives make a positive
But a positive and a negative
Will never make a positive.

Conquer

Just because he broke your heart

Doesn't mean you should be afraid

To love again

You are here to risk your heart

You are here to love as much as possible

Love is just like an other fear

If you don't conquer it

It will conquer you.

<u>You Never Know</u>

But you never know

When you'll walk into the street

And get hit by a bus

Or you'll be sitting in class

And be shot in the head

Or your heart will suddenly give out

For no apparent reason

Or you'll be trapped in the middle of a burning building

Or you'll be driving

And swerve off the road

There are 1,000 possibilities

Of how or when you'll die

And any of them could happen at any moment

So stop thinking about him

Stop thinking about why he left

Or who he left you for

And start thinking about living

Before that bus comes

Or that gunshot

Or that heart attack

Or any other way that death could capture you

Focus on living your life

Living for exhilaration

Not for him

Not for his heart

But for your own

Love yourself to literal death

Because that's the only guarantee you really have

You need to stop breathing for him

Stop blaming yourself for him leaving

And move forward

Because you could die while reading this

Your life could be taken from you

All it takes is one single instant

To either change your pathway

Or to die

So live

Because you simply never know.

<u>You Are Pure</u>

There's gold in your blood

And diamonds in your bones

And I believe that's why

Some people hurt themselves

Because they forget that it's there

And they try to find it again.

<u>The Difference</u>
There's a huge difference
Between loving someone
And being in love with someone.

Do not mix them up.

<u>Something</u>

Heartbreak is one of the ugliest things

I have ever experienced

But it comes from the most beautiful thing

The world has ever seen

And I think that must mean

Something.

<u>In The Movies</u>
People say love doesn't exist like how it does in the movies
But I disagree
They had to have gotten the idea from somewhere
Right?

<u>Impossible</u>

So go ahead and say that you hate me
But I know in your heart that you don't
Because you can't hate someone you used to love
It's impossible.

The Monster

You'll see the monster

Of what he has become.

<u>Don't Blame Yourself</u>

But honey, don't blame yourself

For him breaking your heart

Just because you let him in

Doesn't mean that it's your fault

It just makes you more beautiful

For being pure enough to trust him

The world threw you two together for a reason

And that reason was for you

To gain some passion

And carefulness

And self respect

And that's exactly what you're doing now

Don't blame yourself for that.

<u>Butterfly</u>

I went down by the beach

And disgust crept onto my face as I noticed

A dead carcass of a fish laying on the sand

It reminded me of us

Its middle was split open

And it was covered in maggots and flies

And all the other decomposers of our death and debris

Reminded me of how our love died among the waves

And washed up on the shoreline

And now we are being picked at by repulsive bugs

I can feel them take little parts of me day by day

These decomposers

The ones who make us do horrible things

The ones who make you love another girl

The ones who make me go absolutely insane

I stared for a minute

And then something beautiful came along

A magnificent butterfly

No bigger than a quarter

And it flew through that crime scene as if it wasn't there

It shined of a lovely orange tint

Matching the sun

And it landed right in front of my feet

And I bent down

And I placed my pointer finger right beyond its legs

And it climbed upon my finger and stayed there for a minute or two
And I focused my gaze on this enlightening creature
It was small, yet powerful
It's wings erupted in a soft flutter as it left my skin
And I realized
Maybe there's good beneath the shades of this darkness
The black hole that we're stuck in
That I am stuck in
Maybe there's something more to the death of our love
Than what there seems to be
Maybe that butterfly could be my new beginning
Maybe all I have to do
Is follow it to where it lands next.

Strongest Souls

"Why do bad things happen to good people?"

Because hell tries its best
To breakdown God's strongest souls.

You're stronger than you think.

Fight Your Battles

So who do you want to be today?
The person who walks away
And leaves their soulmate in the dust?
Or the person who faces everything
Because love can conquer all?

<u>Ironic Balance</u>

I think it's funny how sometimes

Hatred turns into love

And love

Turns into hatred.

The Mirror

She looked at me and smiled proudly
"But you ARE special
Not many people
Can turn pain into poetry."

With Or Without You

I've come to realize

That the world is too big

For me to be upset about you

There's more to live for than just you

Because I want to explore the Earth

And I'll do it whether you're by my side or not

There's beauty in the waters connecting us

And the ground beneath us

And the trees surrounding us

You're not the only beauty upon the Earth

Through my eyes

I've come to the realization that I'm here for me

I'm living this life for me

I'm not here to live for you or anybody else

I will swim the crystal shores

I will walk the hollow ground

I will travel throughout the trees

And it's okay if I do it alone

Because the sights are all the same

With or without you.

A Queen

She's a queen

But she forgets it all the time

Simply because she does not always

Have a king around.

Dig

I know what my problem is

I love too hard

I let who I love walk all over me

I physically dig myself a grave

Jump in

And then spend lifetimes

Trying to get out

Don't let my problem be yours

If your heart is anything like mine

Then please

Follow this for the rest of your life.

Dig yourself gardens, not graves.

I Chose Me

I chose me

Because it was the only option that I had left

Someone had to choose me

Because you sure as hell weren't going to

So I chose myself

And I'll continue to choose myself

Again and again

Until someone else is worthy of me.

<u>Open</u>

Open mind

Open heart.

Just know how to close them.

<u>One Single Love</u>

You liked him because he was nice to you

You're going to meet a thousand guys

Who will be nice to you and then leave

But only one of them will stay

And it's not going to be easy to find that one

It's going to be really goddamn difficult

It's going to take a while

It's going to be frustrating

And annoying

There will be times where you feel yourself melting

And times where you want to fall asleep and never wake up

But just remember

That that one is bound to show up

The universe didn't rip

All those loves away from you

For nothing.

Be Mad At Him

I know that you're mad at yourself

For falling for it again

But don't be

Don't be upset with yourself

For having a heart.

Be mad at him

He's the one who tore it apart in the first place.

Good Blood

I've got angels in my blood

You've only got demons in yours.

Big Heart

You're really gonna let him back?
After everything he put you through?
Every lie
Every tear
Every sleepless night
You can't do this
You can't let him walk in
And walk all over you
And you know I'm right
You know you don't need him
You know he's only bad
And yes, your heart is big
But not big enough to let him back in.

He doesn't belong in there anymore.

<u>The Other Way</u>

The hardest part isn't turning around
And walking the other way
The hardest part is to continue walking
Without turning around.

<u>Stop Trying</u>

If they won't even attempt

To listen to you

Then don't give them anything

To listen to.

He Lost All

I just didn't have the energy anymore

To love my only someone

Who split their time and love

Between three people:

Me

Her

And himself.

He lost all of me

While I only lost one-third of him.

Just A Boy

I know that you're in love with him

But sometimes you have to take a step back and remind yourself

That he's just a boy

And within those pretty eyes

And that striking smile

Realize that the love he gives you

Is no more valuable

Than the love you receive

From your friends

And family

And angels

The only difference is a single body part.

Don't let that one, single thing control you.

He's just a boy.

Castles

That's the beauty within everything.

I built castles
Out of the fake love you spat on me.

<u>Tiara</u>

Kill me

I dare you

I'll rise from the dead

With a tiara on my head.

I Will Not

I will not sit around and wait for you

"Maybe in the future…"

Is not good enough for me

If you don't love me now

Trust me now

Want me now

Then you never will

It's as simple as that.

Leave It Alone

It's over

You can't have him

And he refuses to have you

Leave it alone

He's gone

And I know it hurts

But he's not coming back.

<u>Despite All</u>

And despite all the pain

Despite all the people with dirt for hearts

That have ruined me

It's the words that refuel me

The words are the ones that force me to sit outside for hours

Writing countless and meaningless poems

With only one purpose.

To keep me alive.

<u>Be The Water</u>

Don't be the bridge that he walks over

To get to her

Be the water under the bridge

Ever changing, but always beautiful.

<u>All About Control</u>

It's all about control.

But remember
What's even more important
Than having control over him
Is having control over yourself.

<u>She May Be</u>

You fell so in love with her
You treated her like a princess
And gave her everything that you didn't give me
Well newsflash
She may be a princess
But I'm a goddamn queen
And I refuse to let you treat me like anything else.

<u>Too Strong</u>

You left because you got caught
You liked the idea of me being vulnerable
Even though I never truly was
Yes, I had feelings for you
But strength is drilled so deep into me
That vulnerability can no longer reach my heart
So when I found out your past
You didn't like it
You didn't like the idea that you were now vulnerable
And I was not
You wanted to be in control
And I hate to break it to you
But you were never in control
I was always too strong for you.

Not For Him

I'm fighting for me this time
Not for him.

<u>Where Survival Dies</u>

You need to understand

That the feelings between the both of you

Cannot survive under the circumstances that they are in.

                                        Accept that.

What You Choose

You get to choose who you like

But you don't get to choose who you love.

Don't blame yourself for loving them.

Teenage Boys

This is the truth

His heart is with you

But his body's with her

And knowing teenage boys

They're gonna choose their body

Over their hearts.

Fingerprints

I stood in front of the mirror today

With my pen and paper in my hands

Held to my chest

And I looked at myself

And I whispered

"I'm sorry... I still love you"

To my reflection

Hoping to get a response back

And I felt my heart

Stitch itself back together

My eyes

Lighten with accomplishment

And I looked down at my arms

And my hands

And my legs

And I realized something

I realized that I could not

Wash your fingerprints away with soap and water

I couldn't wait for a shooting star to fall upon my eyes

And wish for your fingerprints to disappear

It was so much simpler than that

All I had to do was forgive myself

For thinking that I did something wrong

And accept that the horrid truth

Of how you aren't coming back

Is simply just the truth
There's nothing horrid about it
I smiled a genuine smile
About everything I had been missing about myself for weeks now
I felt the sweet shine of clear skin
Skin that no longer resembled you
Every time I looked at it
Skin that is a part of me
And not a part of you
I let the traces you left behind
Be deleted from my soul
Your fingerprints no longer stain my existence
Every print that you left shattered upon me
Taught me a lesson
Hundreds and hundreds of lessons
Captivated my skin
Not mistakes
Not fingerprints
Not anymore
I can bathe in pure waters now
Without trying to wash you away
I can smile for as long as I want to
Without you corrupting my mind
I can be me again
I can be real again
I can be whole again

I did not need to free myself from you

All I had to do was free myself of you

Let myself move on

Be happy

Live every moment

Every breath

For me

Because in the end

My heart is beating for me

And my lungs are breathing for me

And your fingerprints

No longer sketch themselves on my heart

Or lungs or hands or mind

I am okay with never seeing you again

I have been given an opportunity to restart myself

And you're insane if you think I'm not gonna take it

It's all about control

And you controlled me

Up until I erased you from me

Looking into that mirror

Was the best thing that ever happened to me

And I'm proud to say

That I've officially let you go

I have learned so much

From your fingerprints

So thank you for breaking my heart

And thank you for leaving your disgusting signature
All over my body
Because I was given the honor
Of cleaning it up.

Thank you for taking this journey with me. I hope you enjoyed it. I love you all.

Feel free to follow me on Instagram for updates on more of my possible future projects.

Instagram: trinity_lemm

Thank you again.

Made in the USA
Lexington, KY
06 October 2017